*To my brother, Karl, who opened my ears
and taught me to not just hear music,
but to listen.*

ACKNOWLEDGMENTS

Special thanks to Barbara Wilburn, whose editing skills and encouragement were invaluable.

Thanks to Andy Head for the cover design, and to Kim Head for help with the title. And for all of their support and enthusiasm.

Another special thanks to Irina Feoktistova, who was my extraordinary accompanist and pit pianist for the vast majority of shows I've conducted (until Lyric Opera of Chicago snatched her up). At the end of our first rehearsal together for a production of *A Chorus Line*, this highly trained classical pianist sat at the piano in wonder as the cast gathered their belongings in the house and started heading for the door. She looked over at me, beaming, and said, in her thick Russian accent, "I never played rock and roll!" She giggled. I thought it was so cute that I stopped the cast and announced what Irina had just

Tales & Tips from the Pit

Tales & Tips from the Pit

A Guide to Music Directing &

Conducting for Community Theatre

Kurt Henning

Copyright © 2015
All rights reserved.

Tales and tips from the pit: a guide to music directing and conducting for community theatre / Kurt Henning

ISBN-13: 978-1508458111

ISBN-10: 1508458111

Acknowledgments

said, and they burst into cheers and applause. Someday, they'll make a movie about us.

Thanks to stage director Jack Lampert, choreographer Kirsten Markham, and producer Bob Bierie for our many collaborations; and to stage director Ty Perry, for sharing the roller coaster ride and headline-making production that was *Ragtime*.

Thanks to Karl Henning and Ted Thomas, who taught me to recognize and value tasteful, appropriate drumming.

And a special thanks to the conductors who helped train me (in chronological order): Peggy Morse Lundberg, Vincent C. LaGuardia, Jr., Victor Yampolsky, John Paynter, Robert Harris, Fred Ockwell, and Kevin McMahon. My "toolbox" is well-stocked.

Contents

Forward		i
Introduction		iv
1	The Joys of Community Theatre	1
2	Knowing the Score	3
3	Production Staff	8
4	Auditions	11
5	Casting	21
6	Rehearsing the Cast	25
7	Music and Staging	34
8	Conducting and the Conductor	38
9	Musical Integrity	48
10	Orchestral Considerations	51
11	Rehearsing the Orchestra	67
12	Various Instruments, Part 1	78
13	Various Instruments, Part 2	91
14	Various Instruments, Part 3	111
15	Opening Night	118
16	This I Believe	123
Index		130

Forward

My own experience with music directing and conducting began in high school, when my orchestra director showed me most of the basic conducting patterns one day after rehearsal. I practiced them incessantly for the next few days and caught the "conducting bug." I was hooked. Shortly after that, any time the director needed to excuse herself from a rehearsal, she would allow me to put down my string bass and lead the rehearsal until she returned. I was honored in my senior year of high school to conduct a piece at my final orchestra concert. The piece was Pachelbel's Canon, but the arrangement we were playing was the "Theme from *Ordinary People*," an acclaimed 80's movie. My first executive decision at the first rehearsal was to cut the soft-rock drum part. The drummer was none too pleased, but I just couldn't bring myself to perform Pachelbel's music with a cheesy drum beat. Sorry!

I went on to earn a Bachelor of Music degree in Double Bass Performance at Northwestern University, and stayed on to earn a Master's degree in Orchestral Conducting.

Chicago Symphony Orchestra, here I come, right? But first, I would spend the entire decade of the 90's directing the orchestra and bands at Loyola University Chicago, and act as an assistant conductor for a local opera company called Lincoln Opera, which happened to rehearse and perform at Loyola.

Chicago Symphony, here I co- ! Well, except that in 2000, I took my baton into my local community theatre scene. From 2000 to 2008, I music directed and conducted about 17 different productions for various theatre companies in the Chicago area.

I decided to take a break from doing shows in 2008 and have recently decided to get back into it. In the time that has elapsed, I have been channeling my

Forward

creative energies into writing. I am working on two different projects: a memoir and a screenplay. In my time away from conducting, I have found that when you put something aside for a while, you tend to gain new insights and perspectives on it. So, just as I was deciding to go back to conducting for community theatre, the idea to write a book on that very subject came to mind. Two of my worlds – conducting and writing – collide! And here is the result.

Chicago Symph- ! Well, but first this book.

Introduction

Let me start out by explaining that, due to my own background and training, I regard music directing and conducting as one and the same role: I believe the conductor for a show should be the music director, and vice versa. I recognize that they are often split into two different roles: the music director comes in at the beginning of a production and teaches the cast their music. Later, somewhere toward tech week, the conductor (a different person) comes in with the pit orchestra he or she has prepared, and hitches that wagon onto the production through the end of the run. This book tackles issues that are faced whether those roles are split between two people or handled by the same person. I make this point because I tend to use the terms "music director" and

Introduction

"conductor" interchangeably. In my mind they are, ideally, the same person handling a single role.

Your interest in this book probably lies in the fact that you currently music direct and/or conduct shows for your local community theatre, or you are about to start. I'm going to take an educated guess and say that you teach and/or perform as a pianist or vocalist, or have done a lot of work as an accompanist. The other common path to working on community theatre productions comes from working as a music teacher at the local public school. All of these paths provide a good musical foundation, but none of them actually prepare you for the ins and outs of what you are being asked to do, which is to prepare people from your own community to perform a Broadway show. But who actually takes classes in music directing and conducting *for community theatre*? No one!

Over the last 30 years, I have sat in many an orchestra pit as a bassist and observed first-hand how inadequately we are prepared to do our job when it comes to conducting shows or preparing casts and orchestras for performance. Since no one makes their living conducting for community theatre, it is unrealistic to think that anyone is going to go back to school and take classes to brush up on their conducting skills, or to make an extensive study on popular musical styles and their components from the last 100 years, or to sharpen their rehearsal technique. I would say that 99% of those who currently music direct shows in their community have done all of the formal music schooling they will ever do. This book is designed to fill in some gaps without requiring you to register for classes somewhere and plop down a year or two's worth of tuition. You're already out there doing it or are about to start. Depending on the given topic, some chapters are rather short and perhaps offer only my philosophy or personal take on an aspect of our job, while other chapters delve deeply and very practically into the subject at hand.

Introduction

I can pretty well guarantee that, regardless of your previous training and experience, there are issues in this book that have never shown up on your musical radar before, issues that need to blink brightly and get your attention. Or maybe they have blipped on your radar, but you have not known how to address them or have wondered if it was even your place. In writing this book, I have tried to include every single musical issue I could possibly think of that is routinely overlooked by even the most experienced music directors I've worked with in community theatre (of course, not every issue is overlooked by every music director, and certainly not every issue arises in every show).

So, best of luck with your current or approaching production! May you and your cast break many legs, and may the advice offered in this book help you break them in style.

1

The Joys of Community Theatre

If I could make my living conducting community theatre, I would. My reference to joy in the title of this chapter is not meant to be sarcastic.

One of the beauties of community theatre is how it brings together people of varying ages, abilities, backgrounds, and experience, all working toward a common goal: to present the best show they possibly can. Our job as music directors and conductors is to help them pull it off! It is definitely a challenge (sometimes more than others), but the process of getting there contains a myriad of opportunities for fun, learning, and growth, both collectively and as individuals.

Conducting symphony orchestras and concert bands has its challenges and rewards, but what more magical place to work than the theatre? The lights, the costumes and makeup, the sets and scenery, comedy and drama; rehearsing not only with other musicians, but with actors – a bunch of crazy people! And in both the community theatre orchestra pit and among the cast and crew, you will find yourself working alongside lawyers, doctors, teachers, parents, students, veterans, artists – just about every walk of life you can think of. If you music direct and conduct for community theatre, you are in a very unique place – a place to be appreciated and cherished. Never lose sight of that fact.

2

Knowing the Score

As soon as you land a gig as a music director for a show, the first thing to do is get your hands on the score and learn it. Knowing the music as well as you can even before your early production meetings will help to inform some of the decisions you make at those meetings. And it will be invaluable as you sit through auditions looking for the perfect people to fill the roles. Spend time in the score. Learn the tempos and tempo changes. Figure out as early as possible whatever cuts will be made to the score (in consultation with the stage director and choreographer). Also, in your initial score study, *learn the story of the show* and how each musical number fits into that story. Always keep in mind that, as the conductor for a theatrical production, you're helping to tell a story. You are a storyteller.

In a recent and very positive development, publishers have begun to issue full scores for some of the Broadway shows. If you are like me and coming to musical theatre from the classical and opera world, you will be very happy to hear this. When I first got into musical theatre, I was a bit dismayed to think that I would never again see a full conductor's score. I suddenly found myself in the realm of the "reduced score." For the time being, the reduced score is still the norm, and more often than not you will be stuck with using one. If that is the case, don't bother looking in your score for that instrumental line you're trying to correct at rehearsal. At most, you'll find a reference in tiny print to that instrument's entrance at measure 23, but you are primarily looking at a piano reduction of the score with a few added cue lines.

As you study your score, listen to the original Broadway cast recording of your show and, if available, the movie soundtrack. As you listen to any recording, always bear in mind that you are hearing *an* interpretation of the music, not *the* interpretation. There is no *one* interpretation of any piece of music. Any recording you hear only suggests possibilities. The differences you hear between a movie soundtrack and the original production illustrate this perfectly. As the music director/conductor, you have the final say in the interpretation of the music for your production. In any case, listening to recordings will help familiarize you with the orchestration (nine times out of ten, you will be working with the original Broadway orchestrations), and you can mark your not-very-informative reduced score as needed to help you know when the brass players might need you to throw them a cue.

Knowing your score also helps save you from embarrassing situations. For instance, maybe you're studying the score for your first production of *Chicago*, a show you are not yet very familiar with, and you notice that whoever is cast in the role of Velma Kelly is going to have to hit a high B-flat, because that's what your score says. So, at the auditions, you make sure that every actress who is going for Velma has that note in her range. Meanwhile, the ladies auditioning for the part are all scratching their heads and looking at each other because, being more familiar with the show than you are, they can't recall where Velma ever sings that high. But there it is on the page, in black and white.

After casting the show, you have the girl who's playing Velma come to her first rehearsal to learn her music. You have the pianist plunk out the notes on her first phrase, and the actress is doing that scratching-of-the-head thing again. And suddenly you realize that Velma's vocal music is inexplicably written *an octave higher than it is sung.* You find yourself wanting to call everyone who auditioned for Velma so you can apologize and explain, but you realize it's too late and you have to move on, feeling stupid.

Yes, that was me. The lessons I pass on here come not only from observing other music directors, but myself as well. Though I put a lot of stock in whatever training I've received, it will always be true that "experience is the best teacher." Know your score, and know the show.

3

The Production Staff

The production staff for a show includes the producer(s), the stage director, music director, choreographer, costume designer, set designer, sound, makeup, tech crew, etc. You will primarily be interacting with the director and choreographer. You will also be working with the sound designer, but more on that later.

Here is how I view my role as a music director coming into a production: Yes, I'm supposed to teach everyone their songs – of course. And if I'm also the conductor, then I rehearse the orchestra and help to execute the performances. But beyond that, my deeper role is to help the director realize his or her overall vision for the show, and to help the choreographer achieve his or her goals, as well. I am there to *help*.

A few years ago, I heard about a clash during a rehearsal between a director and music director, and the music director, feeling he was losing the argument, pointedly said, "It's **musical** theatre, not 'stage-ical' theatre!" The implication was that the music comes first above all other considerations.

I disagree. If we look a little deeper, we see that "musical" is the adjective, the descriptive word. The noun here, the thing being described, is "theatre." So, what we are dealing with when we say "musical theatre" is primarily a theatrical performance with the added element of music. It is first and foremost theatre. We, as music directors and conductors, are guests in the theatre world. This is why I maintain that our role as music directors is to help stage directors realize *their* vision.

And once you've worked with any of your local choreographers for more than ten minutes, you will see that your role is pivotal in helping them get their job done. In almost all cases, the choreographer is the best person to set tempos for dance numbers. And he or she is likely going to need some cuts made in the score. Your job is to make sure those tempos are followed and that the cuts make musical sense and are playable by the musicians.

This is not to say that the director and choreographer are there to tell you how to do your job. You are the expert on musical matters, and there are times when you *will* need to stand your ground as the music director (more on that later, too).

Any healthy relationship is going to have some give and take, and your relationships with the other members of the production team should be no exception. The question that should keep recurring in your head is: how can I do my job with integrity and in a way that helps the director and choreographer reach their goals? That is being a team player.

4

Auditions

Have you ever auditioned as a musician or an actor for something? If you have, I hope you remember how it feels to be in that position. For many people, it is terrifying. One of my musician friends described the audition process as: "One of the cruelest things that human beings put other human beings through." And this was not said by a bitter, frustrated musician ready to give up on the dream, but by a guy who landed one of the premier musical gigs in the country.

As I went through my first few musical theatre productions, I began to notice a pattern. During auditions I would be sitting with the director and choreographer, waiting to hear people come in and sing their musical selection. As mentioned in the first chapter, you come across a wide range of ability in community theatre, and this is certainly most apparent during the audition process.

So, there we'd sit, listening to one prospective cast member after another, after another – some great, some okay, some not so good, and some awful. It is what it is. Very often, after a not so good or awful singer finished their song and left the room, the director and choreographer – who in these instances had been doing shows much longer than I – would begin making the cruelest remarks about what they had just heard. And I get it – it's not as if they were saying those things to the person's face. I'd roll my eyes, too, and maybe offer up an insulting comment to fit in. But I felt uncomfortable making those comments because of things I had observed other than just sub-par vocal skills.

First of all, I noticed how incredibly nervous people tended to be standing in front of us, with

Auditions

nowhere to hide. And I had to assume that they truly wanted to do their very best, that they wanted to impress us; that they sorely wanted to make it into the show. It also occurred to me that no one was forcing them to go through this ringer we call an audition, which again speaks to how much they desire to participate in the upcoming production.

I was scratching my head, trying to figure out just what motivates people to go through with this, and then I realized the answer was right in front of me as soon as they opened their mouths to sing. Whether possessing the gifts of a Caruso or... or not... there is one overriding reason why people willingly put themselves through one nerve-wracking audition after another, with no guarantee of success: *people love to sing*. And if you think about it, it's not just the people showing up at auditions – it's everyone, all over the world, for as long as there have been people. Singing is in our DNA; it is part of who we are.

At musical theatre auditions, people get up to sing in front of three other people whose sole job is to *judge* them. They stand up there for one reason, and it is a great one, perhaps the greatest: love.

Once that hit me, I had to respect *everyone* who climbed the stairs onto that stage. Regardless of ability, I began to enjoy watching my fellow human beings summon up the courage to get up there and try. Suddenly, instead of looking at people through a jaded eye, I regarded every one of them as noble and heroic in a way, not because of their ability, but because they were *trying*. Another part of our DNA is that we love to watch people who are striving for something, whether they are Erin Brockovich, Walter Payton, Itzhak Perlman, Harriet Tubman, or little Sally at her first (or tenth) audition. There is beauty in striving, and I see that beauty in everyone who stands in front of me to sing a song.

This respect for all who are auditioning compels me to do what I can to put them at ease before they sing. I know that the more comfortable they feel, the better they will do. Use your sense of humor – laughter is a great stress reliever. If you can knock down that invisible wall between you and the person about to audition with some silly or reassuring comment, do it!

One of my prouder moments concerning putting (or keeping) people at ease came one night at an audition when a young lady presented her sheet music for our accompanist. The particular stage director for this production liked to have groups of people on stage at the same time, so behind this young lady stood a bunch of other people who had already sung or were still waiting to sing. I was standing next to the accompanist, and as the young lady handed me the music to put on the piano music desk, I asked, "What is your tempo for this?"

She looked at me and said, "I think it's in G."

I quickly scanned the music, pretending to confirm her statement, and as if she had just answered my question, I said, "Yes. Great! And how fast do you take it?"

As she tapped out her tempo, I noticed an actor on stage with whom I had worked before. He was looking at me with a huge grin. I took his smile to mean, "Really? 'I think it's in G'? What a dork!" Later, he approached me and said, "I just wanted to tell you how great I thought it was that you gave no hint when that girl misunderstood your question about the tempo. It was obvious you didn't want to embarrass her and make her uncomfortable. That was really cool." His comment made my night. I didn't do what I had done to be noticed (in fact, quite the opposite – I was trying to be as subtle as possible), but someone caught it and appreciated it.

Auditions for me are no longer about who is great and who sucks. They are about love and striving. Would that we could cast everyone who shows up, but that isn't realistic. For what it's worth, I look upon even the poorest singers, actors, and dancers with the greatest respect. They show up, and they try. Being jaded toward them makes no sense to me.

So much for the philosophical aspect of auditions. There are a few practical things to consider, as well.

Obviously, you need the best sight-reading pianist you can find to play everyone's selections. Find that pianist, pay them for their time, and thank them profusely at the end of the night.

Typically, people are asked to prepare from 16 to 32 bars of a song, which is all well and good. If turnout at the audition is light, indulge them and let them sing those 16 to 32 bars. However, if you have a heavy turnout, you can avoid a late night and a long waiting time for the auditionees if you cut people short. Let's face it, you can usually tell what a person has going for them vocally after about the first four measures. Cutting people short is a real time saver, but there is a way to do it that will not offend people or make them feel cheated. You simply have to prepare them for it.

"Before you get started, I just wanted to let you know that I will probably cut you off a little early, but don't take it as a thumbs up or thumbs down. It just means I've heard what I need to hear. We're trying to move a lot of people through here, so we won't have time for the whole selection." Then I smile to look friendly.

Once they're on board with that, I try to get them to start eight measures or so before the climax of their selection so they can hit that note they're dying to sing for me. If the range of the part they are going for isn't particularly challenging (perhaps they just want to be in the ensemble) and they don't need to hit "that note," or if, due to inexperience they find it difficult to start anywhere but at the beginning of their selection, I start them at the beginning and then cut them off at about the eight measure mark and thank them very kindly. Though it may disappoint

Auditions

some to have their song shortened a little, if you do it gracefully, people will leave feeling like they did what they came to do.

Some music directors (and stage directors, for that matter) don't want to hear people singing songs from the musical for which they are auditioning. I guess the reasoning is that they don't want people bringing in a prior interpretation of the music or the role that the production staff might be stuck with and can't mold or shape to their liking if that person is cast. Personally, what people sing at the audition makes no difference to me, provided that it is at least within the same genre as the show, or close to it. I want people to come in singing whatever they feel will put them in the best light vocally. If that means singing a song from the musical we're going to produce, so be it. And I have found people to be remarkably flexible when it comes to reworking a song (or a role) away from a prior interpretation, but maybe I've just been lucky in that.

If a role has an especially high (or low) note, and you know it isn't due to an errant score, make sure the people going for that role have that note in their wheelhouse. You can quickly check by having them sing three or four scales that take them up (or down) to that note. More experienced singers (refer to their resume if provided) can simply tell you what their high or low note is without singing scales. (See thoughts on vocal ranges as they relate to casting in the next chapter.)

In short, be kind and encouraging to every poor, nervous soul who shows up to your auditions, and help them relax as much as they can by fostering a fun and positive atmosphere.

5

Casting

Bottom line here is: cast the show, not your friends. Your job as the music director is to help produce the best show you possibly can. "The show's the thing." You and the director and choreographer must have the objectivity to cast the people who best fit the roles. This is not the time to be sentimental. Do your job. Your *true* friends who might audition will respect your decisions regardless of the outcome. And if a good friend happens to be the best fit for a role, bonus! But keep in mind that everyone at the audition is counting on your integrity and objectivity. Everyone should have a fair shot.

The most interesting thing to me about casting is balancing the acting, singing, and dancing abilities of each prospective cast member. Maybe the guy with the best singing voice has the acting ability of a tree stump. It will be better overall for the show to cast the guy who acts great and sings okay, who can really sell a tune through his character. Even speaking as a musician, I'd much rather hear an okay voice with solid acting that makes me believe the character, than a polished voice coming out of a zombie. Remember, the theatre is not the concert hall. Theatre is telling a believable story.

If a situation arises where you and the director and choreographer feel that someone is absolutely perfect for a role but that they don't quite have the vocal range the role requires, the pit orchestra (and rehearsal pianist, which might be you!) can be asked to transpose the music to fit the singer's range. It's a pain in the rear, but it is an option. Some scores actually come with some of the songs in two different keys for that very purpose.

Casting

I am reminded of the time I played bass for a production where the orchestra had to transpose some of the music down a little for one of the female leads. A male lead observed this at one of the rehearsals, and I saw a sudden glimmer in his eye that wasn't there before. I could see his wheels turning and thinking how cool it was to have an entire orchestra change their parts for a vocalist, so on a whim he asked the conductor if his songs could be "taken up a half-step." There was a pause as the conductor mulled it over.

Surely, I thought, *the conductor, with his classical training, has noticed that this actor's songs are already straining the top of his range. Surely, the conductor is hesitating to answer because he doesn't want to let the actor down, but he wants to make it look like he gave it some serious consideration. Surely, he'll think of a way to let him down gently. Why am I getting that sinking feeling?*

For reasons I still can't fathom, the conductor agreed to have the orchestra take the actor's songs up.

Predictably, this forced the actor to sing much of his songs up in his head voice, which made the songs sound weak and empty – not at all what you want for a role that is known for its high testosterone level. But he got to tell his friends that the orchestra took his songs up a half-step, and we can only assume that the look of wonder and adulation in their faces was worth it.

Don't be "that conductor." If a suggestion by an actor is musically inappropriate, just say no. And smile.

6

Rehearsing the Cast

The most important thing you do as a music director and conductor is rehearse. Here are some tips to make rehearsals with the cast as efficient and productive as possible.

Scheduling: Generally, when scheduling people for rehearsals, schedule the largest number of people to the smallest. As the rehearsal progresses, you want to keep sending people home as their part in the rehearsal comes to an end. Nothing kills morale like having a bunch of people waiting around doing nothing while you work with two or three cast members. Have those two or three arrive later in the rehearsal as you cut everyone else loose. This should be an overarching goal, though at times this will not be practical, especially the closer you get to tech week.

Warm ups: If you are not comfortable leading the cast in vocal warm ups at the beginning of a rehearsal, chances are there is someone in the cast who studies or teaches voice and would be glad to lead the warm ups for you. Otherwise, get advice from people who do it regularly and adopt some of their routine. Occasionally, someone in the cast might tell you that your warm ups aren't meeting their needs (though they may not put it so diplomatically). In that case, I usually ask the person to teach me an exercise that they particularly like, or I suggest that they warm up on their own as they drive to rehearsal.

Teaching people their music: Singing parts to cast members and having them sing it back to you is quicker than playing the notes on the piano and having them sing their part back. You don't have to be a trained vocalist (i.e., have a pretty voice) to do this. It's about conveying to them the pitch and the rhythm of the words. If you can carry a tune, I would suggest using this method as much as possible. Of course, if someone asks to hear a part plunked out on the piano, oblige them; and at times, for absolute clarity on something that keeps getting missed, use the piano. But for getting through large quantities of music quickly, I've found that nothing is faster than singing to them and having them sing it right back.

At the second or third vocal rehearsal for a production of *A Chorus Line*, I was asking the tenors to review a spot in one of the songs when one of them stopped me and said, "Wow, you actually want us to sing our harmony, don't you?"

I was a little confused by the question and quietly said, "Uh, huh."

The tenor explained: "It's just that most music directors don't teach us the actual harmonies. They're usually like, 'So, sing this for me everyone,' and we sing it, and however it comes out, they say, 'Okay, moving on, sing this back to me,' and we do, and they're like, 'That's fine. Moving on.' They never go back and correct anything or actually teach the four-part harmonies. But you really want us to do it!"

"Well, it's right there in the music," I said, a little defensively.

Smiling, he said, "I know, and it's great!"

The lesson here, music directors, is that it should not come as a pleasant surprise to the cast when you merely do your job. Teach people their parts, and hold them to what you've taught them. Be the director of the music.

Enunciation: As you teach the cast members their music, it is important to stress good enunciation so that what they are singing is clearly understood by the audience. One word of caution on this: please avoid the quasi-comical trap of what I call "uber-diction." What is "uber-diction"? To put it most succinctly, if you are increasing the number of syllables on a given word, you are using uber-diction. "Any dream(muh), any dream will do." You know what that sounds like to the audience? "Dreammuh." It sounds like overkill(luh). Getting the point(uh)? I call it "quasi-comical" because it comes from good intentions but gives poor results (which I somehow find slightly amusing, maybe because I'm evil). Words don't sound clearer just because they're made to sound weird. The average human ear and intellect will pick up the words just fine without exploding that "m" on "dream." It is true that good enunciation involves certain exaggerations or stresses on words that are different from common speech, but if the final product *sounds* exaggerated and completely unnatural, then you've obviously gone too far. Avoid extremes – avoid uber-diction.

Musical integrity: It is especially important for your leads to know that the way people are singing on the radio today and the show they are working on with you are (in almost all cases) not the same styles. Sure, if you're working on *Rent*, *Wicked*, *Legally Blonde*, or *Jesus Christ Superstar*, then singing in a pop style is legit. But if your Laurie (*Oklahoma!*) is feeling "held back" because you're not allowing her to release her inner Beyoncé, calmly let her know she can find solace with the pit drummer, who is not being allowed to let out his inner Buddy Rich. Part of your job as the music director is to teach, when necessary, musical integrity, and you can never apologize for it. Anyone who wants to take their awesome pop vocals with them wherever they go should not be auditioning for the classic Broadway shows. If a singer is having a hard time getting on board, approach it as an opportunity for them to expand their chops – you're not holding them back at all, you're helping them develop as a more mature, versatile performer. Help them discover the beauty and power to be found in singing a gorgeous melody with simplicity and honesty, with sincere, heartfelt, wonderful lyrics. Do not allow anyone in the cast to sing stylistically outside of the show – in that sense, they have the same musical limitations on them as anyone who's playing in the pit.

Adding movement to the music: Know that everything you taught the cast at their music rehearsals will mysteriously disappear when they add the choreography – don't panic, it always comes back! I've seen many a music director start berating the ensemble as the choreography is put into the mix because it doesn't sound like it did at music rehearsals. Don't waste your breath and time. They still know the music, and only repetition with the choreography will bring it back – repetition, not yelling and insults. You will still need to remind them to take a breath here, give a clean cut-off there, support their sound, and make other tweaks. But don't waste the choreographer's time by thinking you have to stop and teach everyone their music again because when they're all moving around the stage learning their steps, it doesn't sound like it did when they were all sitting next to each other holding their music in front of them. Repetition is the key. The music *will* come back.

Don't talk over everyone's head: You likely have formal training in music, but try not to let it show. For example, let's say you have a situation where the sopranos are suddenly confronted with a B-flat, but the music is in the key of C! Realizing the composer is probably giving us a classic V7/IV situation, you want the sopranos to sing a little on the low side of the B-flat so it resolves nicely to their next note, which is, of course, A, the third of the IV chord (F). The way to effect this is to *mention none of that to the sopranos* and just say: "Sopranos, a little lower on that B-flat, please. Have it lean a little toward the A." That is all they want or need to know! Do not bore them and waste their time as you go into the mysteries of music theory and voice leading and pump yourself up in front of them. Some in the cast (who've had some training) will know why you want the B-flat a little flat – the rest don't care, and that's

Rehearsing the Cast

fine. Let them not care! Teach people only what they need in order to successfully perform the show. If you want to give your cast a formal music education, be fair to yourself and to them: set up individual appointments for those interested and charge by the hour. But leave all that "A is the third of the IV chord which in the key of C is F" jibber-jabber out of your rehearsals.

Work hard and use time wisely as you rehearse, but have fun: It's music – it's theatre. People should be having a good time! Rehearsals should be like a solid workout session: when it's over, people are tired, but they feel good.

7

Music and Staging

If you haven't had any experience performing on stage as a cast member in a show, I would encourage you to seek out the experience. I have found that stage experience can inform some important decisions as a music director.

I was working on a Gilbert & Sullivan operetta a few years ago. We were rehearsing the Act 1 Finale and adding the choreography. Everything was going great until we got to the musical climax of the number. At the very height of the music, almost everyone in the ensemble was in the middle of a turn which had them briefly facing the back wall – right when I needed them facing full front. I should hope it would have caught my attention without having had previous

Music and Staging

stage experience, but I feel that, having been on stage in the past, I am much more in tune with staging than I would be otherwise.

Upon seeing the problem, I gave a huge cut-off and asked the cast to hold for a minute. I walked a few feet back from my music stand to where the director and choreographer were seated and asked for a change in the choreography that would support the climax of the music.

Before the smiling and seemingly accommodating choreographer had a chance to say anything, the director blew up and said, "It's musical theatre! There has to be movement!" (As if I had just asked for a "stand and deliver" pose.)

We locked eyes for a moment, my purposely neutral expression contrasting with his look of momentary rage. I looked down at the floor and gave a quiet, "Hmm."

I walked back to my music stand and we picked up where we had left off. A few measures into the music, I felt a hand on my left shoulder. The director leaned in toward my ear and said, "I'm sorry. We'll make a change." I smiled.

In one of the four productions of *Damn Yankees* I've worked on, I noticed at a rehearsal that the Devil had been instructed to make his entrance on stage at the climax of the song "Whatever Lola Wants" (Lola's big vocal entrance after her dance break). Having performed on stage as an actor, I had learned some important things about "stealing focus," which is doing something on stage that draws focus away from what the audience *should* be paying attention to. As soon as I saw the Devil enter at that spot in the music, I knew it was wrong. Every eye in the audience would shift over to the Devil right then and there. I explained to the director the importance of that moment musically, and he agreed that the Devil should enter a little before or a little after Lola's declaratory, "I always g-e-e-e-e-e-t what I aim for!"

Let the audience drink that moment in with *no distraction!*

Staging, music, and choreography all have to work together. Experience up on stage can give you some valuable perspective as a music director, and could help you catch glitches like the ones I've described. And, hey! Good luck at your audition!

8

Conducting and the Conductor

The first part of this chapter would be better given as a conducting seminar, where I actually show you the things I'm talking about. In any case, if you are going to conduct the show you are working on and haven't had formal training as a conductor, here are some questions you need to ask yourself.

Do I know the basic conducting patterns for the various time signatures? And do I know when it makes sense to switch from conducting in four to conducting in two (and vice versa), or to go from conducting in three to conducting in one (and vice versa)?

Do I have basic independence between my hands? Can one hand keep time while the other throws cues or conveys dynamics?

Experienced musicians only want *one* prep beat before they come in at the top of a song, not a whole, silent measure of four or three or two. How can I indicate the proper tempo and character of the music in a single gesture?

How do I start music that has a pickup note? (Here is the exception to what I just stated about using a single gesture.)

How do I convey tempo changes to the musicians and singers that are clear every time?

It's easy to land on a fermata in the middle of a song, but how do I come out of it without throwing people off?

It's also easy to get into a vamp, but how do I get out of it and keep everyone together?

Other items in your job description include: accounting for every beat of every measure in your conducting gestures; "marking" empty bars so musicians who are counting rests know what measure you are on at all times; avoiding any extraneous motion in your hands and arms that might send the orchestra confusing signals; modifying the position of your arms when throwing cues to the orchestra or to people on stage. Shall I go on?

If reading through all that felt a little intimidating, good! It means you still have some things to learn as a musician, and that's okay. I would strongly encourage you to study with someone who is conducting at a local college or who leads a community orchestra or band.

Most of my observations of community theatre conductors come from having played under their batons as a bassist. And, truth be told, much of the good that happens under the batons of untrained conductors happens not *because of* them, but *in spite of* them. Human and musical instincts kick in and the musicians in the pit figure out a way to pull it off, to avoid the numerous train wrecks that would have occurred had they actually *followed* the conductor. I wish I could say that this is an exaggeration, but it's not. It happens constantly. This does not mean that these conductors are stupid sub-humans. It just means they lack training.

A quick word for those who conduct from the piano: First of all, you are doing two different jobs simultaneously and should be paid for those two jobs. If you are not, you are being taken advantage of. Secondly, if you play the piano without having to conduct, you will do a much better job on that piano. If you conduct without having to play the piano, you will do a much better job conducting. If a pianist can be hired to play in the pit, do yourself and the orchestra and cast a favor and use your hands to conduct the show. You will be amazed at how much more expressive you can be playing that magnificent instrument we call the orchestra, at how much more control you have, at how much cleaner and confident the sound of the orchestra becomes. Playing the piano is an art and conducting is an art. They were never meant to be done at the same time by one person, and when they are, both arts suffer. Try it out. Get that "conducting bug" and you'll never go back.

Enough about the physical aspects of conducting. Let's talk about the conductor as a person, as someone with whom the cast and orchestra have to interact.

The stereotype of the conductor is that of the "Maestro," the all-powerful, all-knowing, male God of Music. His grey or white hair flows wildly about his head as he magically elicits glorious strains of music from his minions. In rehearsal, he is screaming, yelling, all but beating his underlings toward the one goal of Musical Perfection. He is stubborn, passionate, persuasive. He is never wrong.

It was during my formal music studies after high school that I came to completely reject this image of the conductor. It turns out that conductors are mere mortals, everyday people who have faults and insecurities just like everyone else. Even *they* put their pants on one leg at a time.

Fortunately, that old-school breed of conductor is dying out, but there are still some who wield the baton and try to live the dream of the all-powerful, tyrannical Maestro, imagining themselves more akin to Lord Voldemort with his magic wand than a musician who has been called in to *help* put a show together. When I run across these conductors, I say that they suffer from "Toscanini Syndrome." To be sure, there are also directors and choreographers and producers who suffer from the same malady – basically, anyone who works on a show that you might identify as a "screamer."

But we're talking about the conductors. You see a lot of memes on facebook and hear stories in the news sometimes about how music is thought to make people more intelligent; it "soothes the savage beast"; it turns our children into happy little Mozarts; it ennobles and elevates humanity. Yet, so many of the people who are considered to have reached the pinnacle of musical talent, knowledge, insight, and achievement – the conductors – have been some of the most belligerent, conceited, self-absorbed, abusive, tantrum-throwing brats! How does that square with all the positive effects music is supposed to have on the human soul and psyche? The highest achievers in the musical realm are mad tyrants?

Toscanini and his kind have historically been excused from their unprofessional, cruel behavior on account of their "artistic temperaments." Again, the most enlightened "artists" somehow have permission to treat their fellow humans like so much trash? Something is off.

I observed during orchestra rehearsals in college that, whether a conductor used humor, belittlement, or a simple, neutral instruction to make corrections among the musicians, the problem was always fixed. The method didn't really matter. What this told me is that, by and large, performers *want* to do their best by default. And that makes sense, because no performer wants to look bad in front of his or her peers or in front of an audience; no performer wants to be embarrassed. Performers in rehearsal are naturally primed for taking correction and fixing mistakes.

This fact alone makes a conductor's tirades meaningless. A neutral instruction or a playful ribbing will fix a mistake just as well as the use of a whip and a chair, so why not use the positive approach? Why not treat your fellow performers with the respect they deserve as human beings?

Those who are still enamored of the good old days will say, "Oh, but listen to the results! Toscanini was a genius!" Really? I have yet to hear one recording conducted by Toscanini that floored me. This is not to say he was a hack, but even if I thought a recording of his *was* spectacular, knowing the abuse and tantrums that were doubtless a part of the process in the making of that recording, knowing that if one of his musicians looked at him the wrong way he'd be fired on the spot, knowing the humiliation some of the musicians had to suffer in rehearsals to reach some fictional state of perfection...

No, it would be like admiring the craftsmanship of a designer suit you knew was made in a sweatshop. You can admire the craftsmanship – it's right there in front of you, undeniable. But at what price?

Now, have I ever lost my temper as a conductor? Sadly, yes. The worst case was where the music director for a production had to transition to the role of pit pianist when I came in to put the orchestra together. Let's just say that his transition didn't go very well. Let's also say that he couldn't let go of the reins and kept undermining me in front of the cast and the rest of the orchestra. And let's just add that one day I'd had enough and blew my top. Unfortunately, my anger was misdirected and I blew up at the wrong people, for which I later apologized. What a ride *that* was!

As I have matured as a musician and as a person, expressions of anger or exasperation have become much fewer and farther between, to the point that I don't remember there being any outbursts in my last several productions, as there shouldn't be. Perhaps I am allowing music to have those positive effects on me that it's supposed to have.

9

Musical Integrity

Probably the first thing that hit me when I started playing bass in community theatre pit orchestras was a lack of understanding among the conductors where musical integrity is concerned.

Musical integrity is that thing that makes music sound, well, the way it's supposed to. Almost 30 years ago, I showed up for the last couple performances of a *South Pacific* production as a sub in the pit orchestra. It struck me as very odd that the drummer was playing rock beats throughout the show – not intense, heavy metal rock beats, but more of a soft rock style.

The beat first showed up during the Overture, and I was flabbergasted. It's not as if the show had been "modernized" and set in the 1970's instead of the 1940's. No, that didn't explain it. I looked at the conductor when I first heard this out-of-place drum beat thinking that maybe the drummer was just messing with her and she'd shoot him a look, at which point he would go back to playing the simple 2-beat that the music required. Nothing. The conductor looked as if everything was just fine. Nothing to see, here. Nothing to hear, here.

Have you ever heard "Some Enchanted Evening" performed as a soft rock ballad? It sounds, well, cheesy at best. It's out of place, especially during a performance of the actual show! *It's the wrong style.*

And there's the word that basically sums up musical integrity: style.

You probably enjoy many styles of music, or maybe just a couple. You are able to enjoy those styles over time because the artists you like keep playing and singing their material the same way.

They're not playing and singing the same *thing*, but what they do sing and play is done in the same *way*, or style, that their other songs or pieces are done. You recognize style in every type of music you hear. And it isn't just one big thing that constitutes a style – it's a lot of little things that, when combined, add up to a certain recognizable style.

It's no different in musical theatre: every song and big dance number in a show is written in a certain style. Our job as music directors and conductors is to respect those styles and see that everything that is played in the pit or sung on stage fits the given style. This is musical integrity, and it is sorely lacking in community theatre. And this is probably what contributes more than anything to that "sound" that is so often recognizable in community theatre, the sound that says, "We're amateurs." But it doesn't have to be that way. I've addressed this some in "Rehearsing the Cast," and will address it in more detail as the book progresses.

10

Orchestral Considerations

*Real vs. Fake – Reduced Orchestra –
Orchestra Placement – Balance –
Sound Guy*

As the conductor for a show, the orchestra is your "instrument." You need to know how to play it, and there's more to it than just beating time and indicating *loud* or *soft*.

Are Those Real?

Up until tech week, rehearsals are typically accompanied by a pianist. When the orchestra is brought into rehearsals, the conductor takes over the role of accompanist and, as just stated, his or her instrument is the orchestra. Let's take a look at that instrument.

Your instrument is, obviously, made up of many instruments. The first thing we need to consider is: are those instruments real or fake? When it comes to a choice between something that is real and something that is fake, people typically prefer the genuine article. Fake trumpets, or real? Fake woodwinds, or real? A fake piano, or a real one?

The performance of musical theatre (and opera) is a very complex, organic, and amazing undertaking which is accomplished through the coordinated efforts of a variety of dedicated artists. One of the most amazing aspects is found in that word, organic. By and large, the things that combine to pull off an impressive show are pretty low-tech: you need a stage, some costumes and makeup, sets and scenery, some sort of light so the audience can see what's going on, writers, composers, actors, and musicians. A musical theatre performance (in the traditional, *not*-landing-a-helicopter-on-the-stage sense) isn't much more complicated than the little dramas Mark Twain's daughters used to perform in their living room, or any production you were a part of in grade school. In community theatre, we are accustomed to using real lights and costumes, real actors using their real voices, and real musicians playing real instruments, with the exception – very often – of what could be considered the backbone of the entire production: that lowly workhorse, the piano. This most significant ingredient, central to virtually every American musical, is now usually fake. Any so-called piano that has to be plugged into the wall in order to work is a fake piano.

I could spend a lot of time writing about the difference between using a piano or an electronic keyboard, and no matter what examples, comparisons or analogies I use, no matter how many pages I fill, someone out there is going to say, "Well, it sounds close enough." End of argument.

The next time you go downtown to hear someone performing Beethoven's Piano Concerto No. 4 (my favorite!), note what the pianist is playing on. It won't be something that you plug into the wall. There is one reason for this: an electronic keyboard does *not* sound close enough.

If the production company you're working with can give you the option between using a (well-maintained) piano and a keyboard, by all means choose the piano. In the context of its use with other acoustic instruments and the human voice, it's the best fit.

Reduced Orchestra

It is rare anymore to find community theatre orchestras that number in the double digits, and I have some advice on instrumentation when you're dealing with a reduced orchestra.

The absolute smallest pit orchestra is the pianist playing from the piano/vocal score.

Amazingly, and due to the inherent awesomeness of the piano, this can actually work. But if the producers want a bigger sound (and they usually do), here is how to build it up from there.

Consider the trio of piano, bass, and drums as the central core of any reduced orchestra. This trio is the rhythm section, the heartbeat of the orchestra. When using a reduced orchestra, *keep the pianist on the piano/vocal score.* If the budget allows for a fourth instrument, I would add the first Woodwind book (which usually has a player switching between the piccolo, flute, clarinet, and possibly oboe or alto sax). If you can add more musicians, I would put in Trumpets 1 and 2. (If you are going to use trumpet at all, *never use just one.* More on that in a later chapter.) Still have money in the budget? Trombone 1. This 7-piece group we have now formed (Woodwind 1, Trumpets 1 and 2, Trombone 1, Piano, Bass, and Drums) is obviously less expensive than a

30-piece orchestra, but it can pack a big punch. From here I would add, as the budget allows, in this order:

Woodwind 2

Trombone 2

Woodwind 3

French Horn 1

Percussion (tympani, mallet instruments, etc.)

Woodwind 4, and so on.

I never start adding strings until the group gets at least up to French Horn 1 (that's an 11-piece with rhythm section and the beginnings of woodwind and brass sections). Again, the pianist is on the piano/vocal score in all of this, acting both as part of the rhythm section, as well as filling in gaps in the orchestration and fleshing out the harmonies. In the 17 shows I've done, I have never used an electronic keyboard to provide fake woodwind, brass, or string sounds. Every sound coming from the orchestra is organic. (The only exception was at an outdoor theatre where I unfortunately had to use a keyboard as a piano substitute.)

Through trial and error, I came to settle on the 7-piece instrumentation mentioned above as an ideal minimum for reduced orchestra. The key to sounding bigger than we are is found in playing together and playing in tune. One night, shortly after a performance of *Damn Yankees* with this 7-piece group, a woman who is active in community theatre as a director and choreographer peeked into the orchestra pit. She looked a little surprised as she peered down and said, "I wanted to tell everyone in the orchestra what a great job they did, but it looks like most of them have already left!"

"No," I said, "this is it. We're all right here!"

"You're kidding!" she said, looking around. "It sounded so much bigger!"

Orchestra Placement

Reference to the orchestra pit brings up a very important subject for the conductor: where should the orchestra be placed?

I have played in pit orchestras from every conceivable location in the theatre: in the actual orchestra pit, along the backstage wall, behind a permanent set piece onstage, in front of the stage but over to the far right or left, from within a literal storage closet just off of stage left, from physically below the stage, onstage in plain sight, and in the catwalk (that's up where they hang the lights *above* the stage).

A 300-year history of theatrical productions with musical accompaniment plus my own experience as a conductor, bassist, and actor, tells me that the best place for the orchestra in musical theatre is (may I have a drum roll, please?): *in front of and a little below the stage* (so the audience can see over you).

Orchestral Considerations

At the beginning of that same production of *Damn Yankees* just referred to, the production staff (minus myself) had already decided that the orchestra would be along the backstage wall. They said that they'd tried having the orchestra in the pit, but it "just never sounded right," and they wanted to cover the pit and expand the stage out over it. I got the part about wanting to enlarge the stage and have the actors out closer to the audience, but on the other hand, I had a job to do, and while the conductor's art ultimately deals in the realm of sound, the craft is a visual one.

I explained to the production staff that conducting a show is like driving a really big bus. The conductor decides when the music goes and when it stops, and controls the pace of the music as it moves along. And the best place to put the driver's seat is right in front, where I have the clearest view of the cast, and the cast can see me. From that night on during that production, my nickname was "Bus Driver." They put us in the pit, and at a dinner after the closing performance a woman in the production staff turned to me and said, "We've never had an orchestra sound that good in the pit. Do you think it's the person who's conducting that makes the difference?"

I smiled and said, "I sure hope so!"

Balance

One of the first things you'll hear when you bring the orchestra in to rehearse with the cast is the director sitting out in the house saying, "It's too loud. The orchestra is too loud." You'll hear that a lot. And you know what? The director is right. The problem is that the balance between the orchestra and the singers is rarely corrected as it should be.

There are three ingredients to getting the orchestra to play under the vocals: 1.) Your left palm. The orchestra needs to get tired of seeing it. 2.) The understanding that whenever people who know every word and lyric of the show say it's quiet enough, it probably still isn't. Their brains can unconsciously fill in gaps that they don't *actually* hear, while someone who doesn't know the show and can't fill in the gaps is wishing the orchestra would play more quietly, or that the singers would sing louder. 3.) The orchestra needs to understand that what drives the music in musical theatre and opera is not repetitive rhythms in the orchestra or the melody that soars over them – it's the *words* that are being sung. Remember? We're storytellers. Without this understanding, the volume from the pit that becomes tolerated is the volume at which people in the house can hear that the vocalist is singing – *that* the vocalist is singing, not necessarily *what* the vocalist is singing. There's a big difference.

There is a fourth ingredient which I've alluded to: the little old lady in the back row wishing the singers would sing louder. Singers need to project, but this is an issue that needs to be carefully addressed by our vocal teachers in their studios, as well as by our drama teachers and acting coaches. Few conductors have the expertise to instruct their cast members on how to properly project without ruining a bunch of voices. Vocal teachers? Coaches? Get on it. The condenser microphone is destroying one of the most basic tools of the stage performer's trade.

    I did three Gilbert & Sullivan productions in a church gymnasium that had a stage at one end. The room had a very high ceiling and a hardwood floor – it was a giant box; very live acoustics; easy for sounds to get muddy. I had a 25-piece orchestra and singers with no mics. After recording a couple of our performances, the videographer commented to me that this was the first time he'd ever recorded in that room and had no problem with the balance between the singers and instrumentalists. It was simple: I kept the orchestra truly quiet, and the singers projected (and enunciated). But these were classically trained vocalists, and projecting (and singing without mics) is part and parcel of their training. But any vocalist, regardless of the genre they are learning, should be taught how to project.

The Sound Guy

I'm hearing voices already: "But we use mics in musical theatre. We don't need to project." It's true, we do use mics, and I don't suppose this book is going to send the sound guys packing any time soon. But let's talk about the sound guy for a minute.

Sound guys are great. They are usually very pleasant, very helpful, and sometimes not even guys. If the orchestra is a guest in the world of theatre generally, then the sound guy should be considered the guest of the orchestra specifically – he is the guest of a guest. Let me explain.

For hundreds of years, all sound and balance issues in theatrical productions that used music were handled by, well, everyone who was singing or playing an instrument. It was an organic process. Eventually, it made sense that the conductor would ultimately become the "sound guy." He was in charge of making sure that everyone could be heard.

Technology introduced the microphone and amplification. The opera world rejected the technology, while the musical theatre world embraced it. Consequently, the sound guy started operating in the musical theatre conductor's territory. A big part of the conductor's job – monitoring the balance between the pit and the stage – was being usurped. This was not done maliciously by this new member of the production team, but more incidentally by virtue of his craft. Over time, this produced a dreaded but seemingly overlooked snowball effect – overlooked until it could no longer be ignored.

It is the nature of a sound guy to want to amplify things. He initially amplified the voices to the point where the orchestras had the freedom to start playing louder. So, the sound guy boosted the vocals a little more to keep them above the sound of the orchestra, and, what do you know, the orchestras could play a little louder. Then, even the orchestras started getting put through the sound system, so of course the vocals had to be turned up even more (because singers weren't projecting anymore at this point), which allowed the orchestras to play even louder, and on and on. The situation deteriorated to the point that the Broadway theatres now have decibel monitors in the pits, and if the orchestra exceeds a certain decibel level during a show, they get fined! Because of years of amplification, singers don't know how to project, and orchestras struggle to remember how to play softly.

How can we as conductors restore balance (pun intended) to this situation? We must implore the vocal instructors and acting coaches to teach their students how to project (of course, this may require instructors to seek out some training for themselves if *they* were never taught). When I do a show, I tell the sound guy (very diplomatically, of course) that my job is to balance the vocals and the orchestra. All I need from him is the slightest boost in the vocals, just enough to make a difference. I keep the orchestra below the vocals, so I don't need him to crank the vocals through the sound system. I also don't need anything in the pit put through the sound system, nor do I need a vocal monitor "so I can hear the singers." If I can't hear the vocals without a monitor, then the audience probably can't either. A vocal monitor for the conductor helps create that snowball effect. It allows you to hear the vocals unnaturally loud, which causes you to allow the orchestra to play louder, which makes the sound guy turn up the vocals a little more, etc., etc. Performing as organically as possible creates the best balance. Where amplification is concerned, less is more.

11

Rehearsing the Orchestra

Rehearsing an orchestra is about getting the most done in the least amount of time. Some mistakes to avoid:

Don't mumble. When you speak to the orchestra, always speak so that those furthest away from you can hear you clearly, even if you are not addressing them at the moment. Having to repeat yourself wastes time. Project!

At the very first orchestra rehearsal, don't stop for every little mistake you hear. Most mistakes disappear after the second or third time through a number, because the musicians catch most mistakes themselves and fix them. This first rehearsal with orchestra is about "big picture" stuff. After you begin a number, try not to stop unless there's a complete train wreck or someone miscounts and becomes hopelessly lost. The musicians want to learn tempos and the road map, the "road map" being the placement of repeats and cuts. These things should have been marked in their parts already (by you), and it should be a simple matter of reading the numbers down one after another. If the musicians have questions after a number, they will raise their hands and ask. If there are no questions and there's nothing you need to clarify, move on to the next number. Your goal should be to have the orchestra read through the entire show at the first rehearsal, and if there's time left over, to go back and hit the trickier spots again. It doesn't always work out that way, but that should be the goal.

Don't overlook the logistical aspects of a rehearsal. Make sure the rehearsal space is set up with the proper number of chairs and music stands before the musicians arrive. Musicians like to start on time, and hate sitting around waiting for things to get set up.

(They also like to be let go early, so surprise them with an early dismissal whenever feasible. They love it!)

As you mark orchestra parts with repeats and cuts (while likely erasing the ones from the last musicians who used the parts – grrr!), make sure there is a system of measure numbers or rehearsal letters (or both), so you can easily tell the orchestra where to begin if you are working something out in the middle of a number. Without this, a lot of time is wasted and musicians become frustrated when the conductor is trying to explain where he or she is in the score without having a simple reference that everyone can easily find.

"Um, I'm starting at…let's see…do you guys have measure numbers? No? You see where we just stopped? Let's see…one, two, three, four, five, six, seven, eight, nine…ten…um…eleven measures before we stopped. Do you remember where we stopped? It was, like, after that one fermata, no, the *second* fermata. Let's see, three bars after? It was really like in the middle of that one measure where it says *ritard*. Do we have that marked in the same place? I have that *ritard* marked at, let's see, one, two, three, four..." If this sounds familiar to you, you're probably a pit musician.

Here's how to avoid this classic, time-wasting, morale-killing mistake. Let's assume you have rehearsal letters in the parts and in your score (they're usually printed as consecutive letters of the alphabet set in a square or circle above a given measure, and spaced somewhat evenly throughout the piece). Now let's say you want everyone to start eight measures before letter H. First, say, "Find rehearsal letter H." Wait a beat or two for the musicians to spot it in their parts. When you see that they are with you, say, "Count back with me from H: one, two, three, four, five, six, seven, eight measures. We'll start right there." Everyone in the orchestra is now looking at the same measure in their music. You raise your arms, they prepare to play, and you're off! Very simple, very efficient. The order of the steps is important. Most of the time, you hear: "Count back with me one, two, three, four…eight measures from H." *Now* they are looking for H, and as soon as they find it, someone will inevitably ask, "How many measures?" You tell them. *Now* they are counting measures. See how much time is wasted?

When you raise your arms indicating that you're about to give a prep beat to start the music, you mustn't hold that ready position for too long or your wind and brass players will hate you. If it suddenly occurs to you that you need to explain something else or if you're having second thoughts about starting, drop your arms while you do your explaining or thinking. Wind and brass players try to time their initial intake of air between the time they raise their instruments to their mouths and when they see your prep beat. Holding them in the ready position is just mean. Once you indicate that you're about to give the prep beat, either give it or drop those arms!

"Too many cooks spoil the broth." Don't allow other musicians to run your rehearsal. They can express opinions and ask if a particular passage can be run through again, and it is often a good idea to accommodate that. But there will be occasions when time will not allow it, and the rehearsal has to move forward. It's your call. Also, the pit musicians should not be telling other pit musicians how to play: "You're too loud! You're flat! You're rushing!" That is your job to say. The exception here is when a section leader is advising other members of his or her section, like the first violinist demonstrating staccato for the rest of the violins so it's uniform.

Even without vocalists at orchestra rehearsals (and it's a good idea to have at least two rehearsals with just orchestra), always conduct as if the singers are present. In other words, indicate when the orchestra should be playing softly under a vocal line and when they can play out. Take all sections marked *rubato* or *colla voce* as if you can hear the singer speeding up or slowing down, and lead the orchestra accordingly. Make every reading of a number as consistent as possible.

Call times for musicians for either rehearsals or performances should be no more than 30 minutes prior to the downbeat. I've had conductors set the call time for an *hour* before. It's excessive. Only drummers or percussionists might need more than 30 minutes to arrive and set up to play, but even they often don't. Musicians know how much time they need to set up before the downbeat. Half an hour is typically more than enough time.

There is a specific type of rehearsal handed down to us from the opera world called the "sit-and-sing." It is the rehearsal where the orchestra and cast assemble together for the first time in the course of a production and run through the music. This can be done with everyone in a large common room, or in the performance space with the cast sitting in rows of chairs on the stage. This rehearsal would normally come after you've rehearsed the orchestra by itself once or twice, and before tech week.

In opera, this rehearsal is known as the *sitzprobe*. Unfortunately, the "s" is pronounced like a "z," which makes it sound like everyone has gathered together to look for acne, which is disgusting. Leave it to the Germans, right?

In the case where the music director and conductor are the same person for a given production, and where this person has done his or her job well in rehearsing the cast and orchestra separately, I find that the sit-and-sing is a colossal waste of time. This is not my idea of productive:

Cast Member A stands to sing his song accompanied by the orchestra. Song begins, song ends.

Conductor: How did that feel?
Cast Member A: Fine!

Rehearsing the Orchestra

Cast Member A sits while Cast Member B stands to sing. Song begins, song ends.

Conductor: How did that feel?

Cast Member B: Fine!

Etc., etc.

You will always get this result if you have properly rehearsed the singers and likewise the orchestra. There should be no surprises, no wrinkles or glitches, because everyone knows the flow of each song, everyone knows the road map, you are familiar with the cast and orchestra and they are familiar with you, and you know how to keep the orchestra *under* the vocals. The rehearsal would have been better spent running the songs with the staging which, by this time in the schedule, should have been happening already in your rehearsals with piano accompaniment.

The only time the sit-and-sing is actually useful is when the music director and conductor are *not* the same person. In this case, while the conductor will have attended some rehearsals to get tempos and other important information from the music director so he or she can prepare the orchestra properly, the conductor will need that sit-and-sing to gel with the cast and make sure everything feels "Fine!"

Of the shows I've conducted, there was only one where I was not also the music director. I was a little nervous going into the sit-and-sing – opening night was coming up fast! I was working with high school kids, and I knew I might create a panic if I began running through the songs and things felt way off. The sit-and-sing did its job – we tweaked things here and there and got rid of the wrinkles. I knew I was doing my job when, after the first run of the show with orchestra and staging, I heard not a peep from any of the cast members, or from the cast via the director. Everyone felt comfortable – mission accomplished.

In another production (where I was music director *and* conductor), the cast was a little shocked to learn there would be no sit-and-sing; some of them expressed concern. The night came when we were scheduled to run the show with orchestra for the first time (we'd already been running it with the piano). Some in the cast weren't so sure we'd make much progress that night, thinking we'd have to constantly stop and fix things. We ran the show, no problem. When the rehearsal was over, the cast went about their after-rehearsal business as if it had been just another night with piano accompaniment – not a concern, not a peep. And members of the production staff, some of whom had their doubts, were pleasantly surprised.

12

Various Instruments, Part 1

Piano – Guitar – Bass

I have been waiting with bated breath to get to these chapters on the various instruments. Much of what I am going to share here are the things that community theatre conductors fail to address time and time again. Being the bassist in the pit, I used to get irked at various players who were doing things that, seen from a conductor's viewpoint, I thought were out of place. But then I realized my little attitudes were misdirected. If anything is happening in the pit that compromises musical integrity, the fault lies with the conductor – it's his or her job to hear it and correct it.

I will always remember a particular symphony orchestra rehearsal I was at while working on my bachelor's at Northwestern. I was sitting in the bass section doing my thing, and the conductor stopped the music to address something back in the percussion section. We had just passed a point in the music that called for crash cymbals, and the percussionist who was on that part had duly crashed his shining cymbals together. Sounded good to me! The conductor, addressing the percussion section generally, asked if there were a pair of larger cymbals available. He felt that the pair being used was too bright – he wanted a deeper, darker sound.

Why is that so unforgettable to me? Because it taught me that there is nothing in the orchestra that cannot be tweaked. To me, a pair of cymbals was a pair of cymbals. As a bassist and wannabe conductor, it never occurred to me that you could be picky when it came to crash cymbals. But you can – and if you feel it better serves the music, you must. It's your job. I share this because some of what I say below might sound like I am asking you to step on the toes of your musicians. I am not. Understand that any sound that comes out of your orchestra – *any* sound – is under your purview. If you don't like the way something sounds, even down to the timbre of a cymbal, you must change it if at all possible. *It's your job.*

Piano

Piano: the king of instruments. I don't think that's an overstatement. But even the "king" sometimes needs to be reminded of certain parameters.

The most common mistake I hear being made by pianists in the pit is overuse of the sustain pedal. Some pianists seem to regard it as a foot rest.

The importance of this point is found in the left-hand part of the piano/vocal score. Because a piano/vocal score is arranged in a way to give the singers the fullest accompaniment to their melodies and harmonies in the absence of an actual orchestra, you find that the left hand of the score is providing the

Piano – Guitar – Bass

"boom, chick, boom, chick" rhythm that drives much of the music like a rhythm section (alternating bass note – chord – bass note – chord), and the right hand is often doubling the melody or providing countermelodies and harmonies.

Piano players love their sustain pedal, and so do I. Without it, the piano becomes almost a completely different instrument in terms of what one can do with musical expression. But that left hand serves a very important function both for the feel of the music and for the singers. The music gets much of its forward motion from that "boom, chick" feel, and the singers need to hear those bass notes clearly for purposes of intonation and reinforcing the sense of time. Too much sustain pedal tends to cancel these important functions out – the music becomes muddy.

Often when I go into a new production working with an inexperienced accompanist, I have to do a little training in this regard. If the accompanist tends to ride the sustain pedal, I explain the importance of that left hand and tell them that I need a "drier" sound to keep it clean. This doesn't necessarily mean *staccato* or that everything needs to sound like a march. It's more a matter of not having the bass note bleeding into the off-beat chord and vice versa (unless it's a ballad, in which case it can create a beautiful *legato*). I address this from the very first rehearsal so that by the time he or she is playing with the pit orchestra, it's second-nature.

If you are working with pianists that are new to the art of accompanying, you may find that they have a hard time following your baton. They are not being mean or rebellious; they're just not used to it. It falls upon you to help train them.

I was working on a production of *The Tales of Hoffmann*, and a fresh, baby-faced pianist who was studying at DePaul University came in as an accompanist. We would start a piece and as soon as he had grasped the tempo, his face was buried in his score and off he'd go! What else should he do when the accompaniment is a series of eighth-note chords for the next 30 measures? Well, what if the singer pulls or pushes the tempo a little bit here and there? How are those metronomically perfect eighth notes working out?

So, of course, the piece fell apart about five measures in. This happened a few times, and I came up with a very simple solution for the pianist. I said, "Once the music starts, never assume that you know where the next beat falls." That got his eyes out of the score. Worked like a charm. I use that same line for any accompanist who isn't used to following a conductor.

The only other thing I would say about the piano is that, once the rest of the orchestra joins in, it is a good idea to identify places at certain spots in the score where the pianist can lay out. For instance, an exposed line that the pianist has always played in the right hand might turn out to be a flute solo. Now that the flute is part of the mix, the pianist can *tacet* that line in his or her part and leave it to the flute player. If a swing number has a walking bass line, there is no need for the pianist to play that bass line once the actual bass is in the pit.

If the theatre company you're working for can offer you nothing but an electronic keyboard in lieu of a piano, remember that the sound coming out of the amplifier can be tweaked. First of all, the keyboard itself may have a variety of "pianos" to choose from. Choose the one that sounds best to you. Second, the amplifier should have controls for the bass, mid, and treble ranges. Tweak all three until you have the most natural sound you can find. Listening to the extremes of each of those ranges can help you zero in on that middle ground. I don't include such advice to offend anyone. To some, this goes without saying. But considering that my advice is based on things I have observed over and over again, I figure this must be useful information to others. Very often (observing as the bassist), I find that the first sound to come out of the keyboard amp is the sound you will live with for the run of the show. No effort is made, either by the pianist or by the conductor, to improve it.

Guitar

It is rare in community theatre to work with guitarists, which is a shame. It's a great instrument, and guitarists usually come in pretty stoked to play in an orchestra pit. If you are fortunate enough to be using one, there is a high probability that he or she, like young pianists, will be new to the whole "follow the bouncing baton" routine. It is imperative that you take them under your wing and set them up for success, not frustration. You must patiently train them to keep looking up at you for tempo changes, including the current tempo that everyone is striving to play. Learn quickly at which spots they'll be depending on you for a good, solid cue, and never fail to give it. The biggest problem I observe with guitarists is their getting lost in the score. In other genres they play, whether it be rock or bluegrass or blues, guitarists are rarely counting measures of rests waiting to make their entrance in a tune. By and large, they are used to playing straight through a song from beginning to end. Remember playing in your elementary or junior high band or orchestra? What was the hardest thing about counting a bunch of rests? Not losing count! It is a discipline in and of itself, and any musician who isn't used to it is going to struggle, especially when they are counting rests in music that is frequently changing tempo and/or meter. Help your guitarist feel a part of the team; don't start a number in rehearsal and then leave them in the dust.

What was said earlier about tweaking the sound of a keyboard applies to the guitar as well. If something in the guitarist's sound is hitting you wrong – too muddy, too bright, too loud or soft – work with them to adjust their settings until they are blending in with the group. Don't automatically accept the first sound you hear and figure that's what you get. (This tweaking principle applies to *any* instrument that is put through an amplifier – keyboard, guitar, bass, electronic drums – anything. Tweak that amp!)

Bass

First, what to call it? The electric bass or bass guitar is easy: those are pretty much the only two names we know that instrument by. It looks like an electric guitar.

The other one, the one you stand up to play that looks like a violin on steroids, has about 3 trillion names, of which these are a few: string bass, standup bass, acoustic bass, upright bass, bass violin, bass viol (which is more accurate than "violin," but who's counting?), double bass, contrabass, dog house bass, bass fiddle, bull fiddle, etc., etc. So, if you see one of those names, we're talking about the big cello.

I was carrying my string bass into a theatre for the first orchestra run-through on a production when I ran into the conductor. He gave me a puzzled look and asked why I didn't bring my electric bass instead. "A lot easier to carry!" he smiled.

What can one say except that the electric bass is not the same thing as the string bass? The show I was playing was clearly written for string bass, so that's what I brought.

A few years prior, I had a great time playing *Little Shop of Horrors*. I did notice how easy it was to carry my bass guitar to rehearsals and performances, but the show was *written* for bass guitar, so that's what I brought.

Know whether your show was written for string bass or electric bass, and then insist on that instrument. One does not sound "close enough" to the other to make them interchangeable (despite what some bassists will tell you about how they set the controls on their electric bass to make it "sound acoustic"). Again, go downtown to the opera house to hear *The Barber of Seville*. At intermission, peer down into the orchestra pit and take a look at the bass section. What do you see? The instrument the show was written for, or the one that's easier to carry?

At this point in history, the majority of musicals being performed are written for string bass. Usually, only the shows that are clearly pop or rock-based use the bass guitar (and a few use both). If you get the orchestra parts delivered and the bass part doesn't specify acoustic or electric (it just says "BASS"), there will be some clues in the part that point to the acoustic bass. Any passage marked *arco* means string bass (that means use the bow). Also, if you don't spot *arco* in the part but do see a passage marked *pizz* or *pizzicato* (meaning to pluck the string with the finger), you're dealing with a string bass part (and an arranger who forgot to mark *arco* in the passage that precedes the *pizzicato* section. It happens.). An electric bass never uses a bow, so there would never be a reason to indicate *pizzicato* in an electric bass part – that part is all *pizzicato*.

If you've looked through the bass part and you're still not sure, listen to the original Broadway cast recording. If you can't tell the difference between the sound of an acoustic bass and an electric, you need to listen to a lot more music. In the meantime, have a bassist friend (we all have one) listen to the recording for you, and he or she will tell you. (Note: Do not rely on Broadway "revival" recordings – you might hear an electric bass in a show that was written for string bass, and for that I take the arrangers and conductors in New York to task. Yeah, I went there!)

13

Various Instruments, Part 2
Drums

As I was packing up my bass after a show that had just closed, the drummer paused from tearing down his drum set and said to me: "I just went and thanked the conductor for allowing me to take liberties with the score. I mean, why just play 'boom, chick, boom, chick' all night?"

This chapter, along with addressing a few other issues, is my answer to that question.

* * *

No matter how old or experienced they are, drummers always seem to have a childlike fascination with their drum set and the cool things they can do on it. And though this fascination often gets them into trouble, I find their enthusiasm refreshing. Ideally, drummers will come into a production knowing what cool things they can and should do on their drums *according to the particular show at hand*, and what even cooler things they shouldn't do. However, it has been my observation that many, many drummers get confused on this point, and it is the job of the conductor to show them the way.

This is a long chapter considering that it is devoted to a single instrument. Lest any drummers reading this think that I have an ax to grind, you should know that, though instrumentally I consider myself a bassist, I have a long and deep history with the drums: my first professional gig was as a drummer. I know drums – I can tear them down, schlep them, and set them up like a pro. I once had to fill in on drums at one of my Loyola University jazz band concerts (where I was directing) when the drummer was suddenly unable to make it. Of course it would be the concert where we were performing

Drums

"Sing, Sing, Sing," right? I'm no Gene Krupa, but I am happy to report that it went off without a hitch. This is all to say that my hawk-like observation of pit drummers over the years comes not from some aversion to the drums, but from a *love* for them. I, too, feel that childlike urge to play all the "cool stuff" when I sit down behind a drum set; I am not immune. It is truly a lot of fun to play the drums. I get it.

Now, as to the role of the drums in the pit orchestra, it is so hard to know where to begin. I've been trying to think of a logical order in which to put my thoughts. Not having discovered a logical order, I will proceed with whatever comes to mind first.

"Edelweiss" is not a [bleep]-*ing jazz waltz!!!*

Ahhhh, I said it! I feel so much better! Oh, you don't even know... For me, this book could just end right here. However, I've seen and heard too much, and I must continue.

Actual drum parts in musicals (as opposed to "percussion" parts: tympani, bells, xylophone, etc.)

are a little open-ended for the drummer. The arranger will indicate the type of beat that needs to be played for a particular song (2-beat, swing, mambo, shuffle, rock), but will not then write out every single hit on every part of the drum set. At most, the arranger might provide a sort of sketch version of the beat to give the idea, but it is assumed that the drummer already has these beats in his or her repertoire, and will play them for as many measures as are indicated (along with the dynamics, rests, etc.). But the fact that a part leaves a little to the player's discretion does not mean it is a free-for-all; it is not a jam session. Drummers have a little more freedom in how they approach their part as compared to other instrumentalists, but *everything* they do must be per the conductor's approval.

(Some of the newer musicals coming out have drum parts with the beats written out explicitly through every measure, including the drum fills. It would be as much of a mistake to expect your drummer to play such a part note-for-note as it would for your drummer to interpret the sketch drum parts as a "Night at the Improv." This new trend sounds like an attempt by arrangers to do what conductors have been failing to do – to keep the drummers on task. I would advise the drummer to treat written-out parts just like the more traditional parts – the first measure or two is a sketch. Play essentially that beat for the required number of bars. In the case of fills, unless they are intimately connected with what the rest of the pit is doing rhythmically, the drummer may opt to play them as written, or do fills that are "like" the written ones. It's a sketch – it's a framework.)

But back to the more common, "sketchy" drum parts: There I sat with my bass (my *string bass*, of course) in the pit for a production of *The Sound of Music*. I had already heard some questionable things coming from the drums, but then we reached "Edelweiss."

The conductor, feeling the song sounded a little empty, decided to take the liberty of adding drums to the mix. The fascinating part was not that the drummer decided to take one of his brushes and start slowly swinging on his ride cymbal: *ting, ting, ka-ting – ting, ting, ka-ting*. Obviously, the song is in three and the drummer, at some point in his career, had become familiar with the concept of the jazz waltz. What fascinated me was that the conductor never even looked at him as the song progressed, never shot him a look that would say, "Ha! You're kidding, right?" Nothing. The drummer played it that way at every performance, and I cringed.

"Edelweiss" was written to sound like an old Austrian folk song being performed in late-1930's Austria at a music festival. Musical integrity demands that we not accompany this song in the context of the show in a style that conjures up images of late-1950's Bill Evans on the West Coast. The conductor, on hearing that swing beat on the cymbal the first time, should have thought, "That doesn't fit the style of this music," and should have corrected it immediately. *Everything a drummer plays must fit the musical context of the show.* Having a part that is not strictly notated like the other parts is no excuse.

Drummers should not have the attitude that they are in the pit to show off their chops and play all that cool stuff they love to play. They are there to play *the show*. I recently heard of a clueless pit musician boasting about the great time he and his drummer friend had playing *The Wizard of Oz*. Apparently, the musician got a thrill out of the drummer playing a samba at some point in the show. When I observe or hear of such things, my first instinct is always to blame the musicians – they should know better. But, no, the onus must fall on the conductor. It was the conductor's job to shut down that nonsense and hold the drummer to the music at hand. Remember that pitiful "*South Pacific* meets Andrew Lloyd Weber" I mentioned earlier? Totally the conductor's fault.

The disturbing part of this is that these things are not addressed because conductors are not hearing them, or at least they're not registering as something to be corrected. Or maybe they are hearing such discrepancies and even disagreeing with them, but they don't feel it is their place to tell musicians how to play their instrument. You're not telling anyone how to play their instrument – they know how to play it already or they wouldn't be in the pit. You are telling them how to play *the music*. If the drummer plays anything that doesn't fit the music, musical integrity demands that you correct it. And, again, it doesn't take a whip and a chair or a brow beating. A simple, matter-of-fact correction will do.

If it's beginning to sound like "musical integrity" means you're supposed to be nit-picky, good! That's exactly right! If you're not used to listening to music so critically, let me offer an illustration that will help you understand how very important this issue is.

Drums

Suppose you're at a rehearsal and you notice that one of the actors keeps going into various accents as he delivers his lines – now he's speaking normally, now he sounds British, now he sounds Russian. Nothing in his part calls for these accents, but he goes in and out of them at random because he really enjoys doing them. Wouldn't you find that rather distracting? Wouldn't everyone at the rehearsal consider it unprofessional and undisciplined? Wouldn't it be obvious to everyone that the actor is more interested in showing off than in doing justice to his role and the production? This is precisely what is happening when a pit drummer is playing the wrong drum beat, and the goal of this chapter is to get this permanently on your musical radar. Just as no one would tolerate an actor going into different accents *because he likes to*, so no one should tolerate the wrong style coming from the drums in a given song. In American musical theatre, the drums are the primary voice in establishing a song's style, and the drum beat must be correct. I'll know this book has had its intended influence in the realm of musical theatre when one day I hear of a *cast member* stopping a rehearsal to ask the music director why the drummer is playing the wrong style. *Everyone* in a production should be able to hear such an error, identify the source, and see to it that it is corrected (using proper channels), just as everyone today can hear an out-of-place accent from an actor.

The most common mistake drummers make in the pit is turning a 2-beat number into a swing number. For the drummer, the 2-beat in its most basic form is a simple "boom, chick" pattern. Nothing fancy; nothing elaborate. The beauty of it is its simplicity. It gives the composer a lot of flexibility to do a lot of different things. It is just as useful in ballads as it is in very fast numbers. This beat is used extensively in virtually every musical written since the 1920's.

Drums

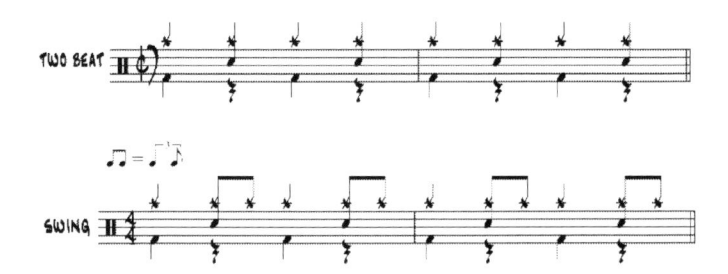

The confusion for the drummer comes from his hearing swinging or lilting rhythms in the other orchestra parts and/or the melody. Often, a swing feel is implied in a lot of 2-beat numbers, but it is a mistake for the drummer, looking at his sketchy drum part, to start playing a full-on swing beat. This locks the music into a swing number, but it's not written to be a swing number. When composers want a swing beat, the orchestrator will write "Swing" in the drum part.

And just as there is a subtle but very important difference between the 2-beat and swing, so there is a subtle but equally important difference between a swing beat and a shuffle. It is not uncommon for drummers, especially in slow to medium tempo swing, to make the mistake of playing a shuffle beat.

Tales & Tips from the Pit

And a slow swing, in the hands of less experienced drummers, is sometimes played as a 12/8. It is your job to hear this and fix it. The only correct drum beat is the one indicated in the score, and composers choose them carefully. Despite their similarities – the swing feel (or an implied swing feel), and the emphasis of the off-beat – these beats are not interchangeable according to the drummer's whim.

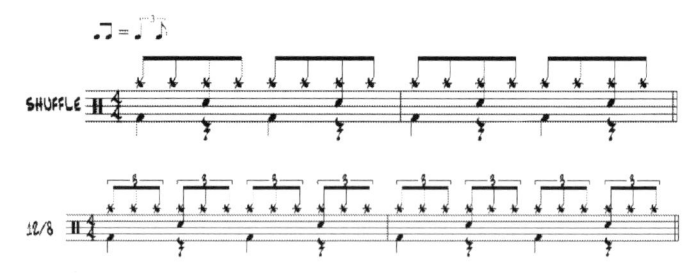

When drummers are first taught the swing beat, their right hand plays the swing rhythm on the ride cymbal, the hi-hat comes down on 2 and 4 with the snare drum, and the bass drum is played on all four beats of the bar. This last detail (bass drum on all four beats) is something more experienced players abandon as they mature musically. No drummer

Drums

worth his or her salt will be found pounding away on that bass drum in a swing number. If your drummer still has this habit, introduce them to the concept of "feathering." As the term implies, the player hits the bass drum on all four beats, but *very lightly*, to the point that if it were to drop out, you may or may not be able to tell the difference. When a swing number has a "walking bass" (where the string bass is playing on all the beats of the measure instead of only on 1 and 3), the string bass is the only instrument that should be heard carrying that very straightforward rhythm if the music is going to flow. Make sure the pianist *tacets* that line in the left hand, and keep that bass drum out of the way.

Many drummers like to take the Percussion part (when a separate player has not been hired to play that book) and integrate parts of it into their drum part. Some conductors encourage this. It is common to see a drummer with his drum set surrounded by a set of orchestra bells, a triangle, wood blocks, and other percussion instruments as he reads out of both books. The main concern for the conductor here is to make sure that the drummer doesn't end up sounding musically schizophrenic. For instance, I have observed many times a drummer launching into a typical 2-beat song doing their wonderful "boom, chick" thing, and suddenly dropping out nine measures in to play a four-note lick on the bells, and then resuming their 2-beat on the drums about three beats later (after they've laid down the bell mallets). Seven-and-a-half measures later the drums are dropping out again so the drummer can play part of a scale on the bells that the pianist is playing anyway. Then the drums come back in. Of course, their hearts are in the right place, but they are shredding the feel of the song by jumping in and out of the drum part. Once that "boom, chick" feel starts in the piano, bass, and drums, it should continue uninterrupted until a big change in the orchestration causes it to drop out of the entire rhythm section. Music is written in sections. If the orchestration changes and the drum part is resting, and a nice passage in the bell part occurs *during* that rest, by all means encourage the drummer to play it. But never have the drummer dropping in and out of a written drum beat to play other percussion parts. It sounds like the orchestrator couldn't make up his mind as to the texture of the song: "I want drums in this song. No, I don't. Yes, I do. No, I don't. Yes, I do."

Musical schizophrenia also occurs when the drummer goes between riding the cymbal and the hi-hat every three, six, or seven measures in a song. As I just mentioned, music is written in sections, and changes in orchestral texture usually line up with those sections. If a drummer is going to switch from riding the hi-hat to the cymbal (or vice versa), and you're okay with the change, make sure he or she is making that change at the beginning of an 8-bar phrase (or 16 or 24 bars), not at some random point in the middle of a phrase. Changes have to make sense musically; they shouldn't occur just because the drummer wants to "mix it up."

One more note in regard to drummers playing lines out of the Percussion book: a floor tom is a terrible substitute for tympani, just as the bell of a cymbal does not a triangle make. Not even close. If the second Woodwind book calls for English horn but the player doesn't have one, would you let the player use a kazoo instead? No. The answer is no.

Another area in which drummers could use some direction is in the use of drum fills. I was attending a performance of *Show Boat* several years ago and generally very pleased with what I was hearing from the pit, when suddenly the orchestra was holding a fermata on the last note of a rousing number (I forget which one) and the drummer started playing the kind of fills you hear on the final chord of a supercharged rock tune – what is commonly known as the "train wreck" ending. You can imagine. It completely lifted me out of the show and into 1970's rock 'n' roll. (How rude is that?) The quickest education here is to simply go back to the original cast recordings and listen to what the drummers were doing – more to the point, what they were *not* doing. And if you can't find the recording of your particular show, it is very informative to listen to recordings of other shows from the same period, shows written in essentially the same style as the one you're working on. The goal here is not to have your drummer sound "just like the record," but he or she should be limited to playing things that fit within the overall style of the show. The basic premise is that you don't want your drummer to be playing things that are "too hip for the room," stylistically pushing the show ahead by a couple of decades or more.

I am not suggesting that shows cannot be "updated" and played in a style different from the original. Who hasn't seen or heard of *Hot Mikado*? I just played a production of Mozart's *Cosi fan tutte* set in 1959 Chicago. This would explain why one of the arias was done as a torch song in a cabaret setting, backed up by piano, bass, and drums. But updated versions have to be produced in a way that is thought-out and coordinated; it has to be done *on purpose*, not as the result of an errant drummer and a conductor who isn't paying attention. That kind of "update" is simply an assault on musical integrity; a clumsy, reckless hijacking of the composer's and lyricist's art.

I can't neglect to share this one – this one is going down in the annals of the misunderstood 2-beat. I was playing bass for *Camelot*. The song was "Guenevere," an epic number that goes on almost forever, and the overall feel of the song is a moderately fast 2-beat, "boom, chick, boom, chick" *ad infinitum* (aside from a militaristic rhythm which comes in near the end). [Note: the song is written in four to correspond with the vocal lines, but orchestrated in a way that makes it feel like a 2-beat.]

The drummer was duly churning out his 2-beat feel, alternating the bass drum with the hi-hat.

Drums

No problem. Out of nowhere, he starts hitting his snare drum at the most god-awful rhythmic interval. Where "snare drum" = the word "CRACK," look at what he created:

Boom, chick, boom, chick, CRACK, chick, boom, chick
Boom, chick, boom, chick, CRACK, chick, boom, chick
Boom, chick, boom, chick, CRACK, chick, boom, chick

I can only describe this in musical terms as a half-time rock beat (some might prefer "back beat"). Whatever you call it, it is so far out of the musical style that it's comical. But because I place a high value on musical integrity, instead of laughing it made me want to tap the drummer on the shoulder and say, "What the hell are you doing?!!" But I didn't. And when it became clear that the conductor wasn't going to say a thing about it, I remembered that my problem was with *him*. I honestly couldn't tell if the drummer was purposely trying to create that feel for some inexplicable reason, or if it was just coming out unconsciously, like farting in your sleep. He would play it at random, at different spots in the song each night, and the conductor had nothing to say.

Pay attention to your drummer.

14

Various Instruments, Part 3

Woodwinds – Brass – Percussion – Strings

Woodwinds

I don't have a whole lot to say about woodwinds, except make sure the piccolo isn't sharp…or flat.

Here's something that applies to woodwinds as well as brass. If all you can hire is Woodwind or Trombone 1, please don't give them the second and third books to pick out important lines from those parts and have them string together a big, clumsy "mega-part" that has them switching books throughout the show. At the community theatre level, we simply don't pay the players enough to take the time and trouble for that. Just have them play out of

Book 1. If there's an important line in the second or third book, chances are the pianist is covering it in the piano/vocal score.

Another thing that applies to both woodwinds and brass: in your efforts to keep the orchestra's volume below the vocals, remember that you must make allowance if the winds or brass are playing in a high register. Most orchestrators know that playing high on a wind instrument requires a lot of air and support, which naturally increases the volume, and they wisely avoid the higher registers when they want a soft dynamic. But in the event that there is a clash between the orchestra and vocals balance-wise, be aware of the register your winds and brass are playing in, and don't ask them to do something that is impossible or next to impossible. Playing soft is hard enough on any instrument, but playing soft *and* high on a wind instrument? You'll have to cut them some slack there. Having them play into the music stand can help, or the brass players can use mutes as a last resort.

Brass

My number one rule for brass is: If you're going to use a trumpet, always use at least two. First trumpet parts in Broadway musicals often require the player to play high and loud. That's a lot of pressure, physically and psychologically. The pressure is made much worse if the player doesn't have that second trumpet part underneath for support. And from the audience perspective, it really doesn't sound so great to have a single trumpet screeching by itself above the rest of the orchestra. It sounds kind of empty and out of place. But that second trumpet part, in addition to supporting the first part, fills out the sound and helps blend it all together.

My other rule for trumpets is to book the best possible trumpet players you can for the money. The trumpet parts are probably the most physically and psychologically demanding parts in the pit, and not having players who are up to the task, who are constantly cracking notes, can be a real buzz kill for the whole show. The quality of your trumpet players can make or break a show. The best ones are always in demand, so the key to booking them is to book them as early as you can. If you wait, they'll already be booked for another show!

Percussion

If your production can afford to hire a drummer *and* a percussionist, then lucky you! It struck me as I thought about what I wanted to say about percussion that, when I see someone I know primarily as a drummer playing the percussion book, they never struggle with that whole musical integrity thing. Percussionists tend to take their tympani and bell and cymbal parts *very* seriously and are paragons of musical integrity on those instruments. They follow the conductor closely, they play their dynamics, they're great at counting rests – they are generally very low-maintenance. Funny how playing the drum set reduces them to that 8-year-old kid who just wants to play cool stuff!

I do have a note about the tympani. These drums are pitched instruments. You wouldn't guess it at some community theatre performances. Make sure before the show starts that they have been tuned to the actual pitches that are called for in the part. If I have found one weakness in the community theatre percussionist, it is in the tendency of getting the pitch "close enough" or "almost there," but it can often be "pretty far off the mark."

Strings

Even though I'm a string player myself and would love nothing more than to work with a string section in all of my shows, I tend to avoid using strings unless the situation is ideal. One problem is that it is very difficult to find really good string players who will play for the going community theatre rates. Maybe it's different in other parts of the country, but the Midwest is Band Country, USA, and finding good wind and brass players never seems to be a problem.

When a production can afford a rhythm section plus some winds and brass *and* strings, I look for the best available and book them as early as possible. You will find that violins are a lot like trumpets: they can make or break a show.

I will not fill out the string section with fake strings (keyboard). It sounds cheesy and says to the audience, "We're on a budget."

Final thought on strings: who told cello players that when the conductor cuts the orchestra off at the end of a number, the cello note – and *only* the cello note, especially if it's an open string – should continue to ring past the cut-off? When did that become a thing? Good ensemble playing dictates that everyone's sound will end together (when not otherwise directed in the score). This practice of letting the note ring after every other instrument is silent has always struck me as just a little arrogant, just a little *prima donna*-like. And it sounds sloppy, like the cellist didn't see the cut-off.

15

Opening Night

Now that you've had your production meetings, held auditions, rehearsed everything to within an inch of its life, and told the drummer to stop it, it's time for Opening Night!

Your first concern is to make sure everything is set up – chairs, music stands, stand lights. From there, you'll want to do vocal warm ups with the cast. While the sound guy is doing mic checks and having someone scramble for fresh batteries for the battery packs, your musicians will be filing in. I would recommend "all black" as the performance dress in the pit. It's classy *and* neutral. Save the tux for wedding gigs.

Opening Night

As the musicians are warming up, you are making sure the tympani are tuned accurately while swapping musician jokes with the percussionist. "How do you know there's a drummer knocking on your door? The knock rushes." "What do you say to a banjo player who's wearing a three-piece suit? 'Will the defendant please rise?'"

The cast will probably have a "circle time" backstage which you will want to be a part of to encourage the troops. If the pianist in the pit has also been the accompanist for the entire rehearsal process, it's a good idea to include him or her in the circle. Your accompanist has been a huge part of putting the show together, and you want to acknowledge that.

As soon as circle time is over, I would send word out to the orchestra (via the pianist if he or she was in the circle) to start tuning. They should be tuned before you make your entrance.

Now you're backstage, the house lights are lowering, and the talkative crowd goes quiet. A spotlight hits where you are about to enter. You walk into the blinding light and make your way to the orchestra as the audience applauds. You motion for the orchestra to rise and the applause grows louder. You present the musicians to the crowd and take a bow. The orchestra sits, the audience settles into silence, you flash the drummer the international sign for "If you throw a rhumba into this production of *My Fair Lady*, I will cut you in half," you smile at the upright bass player because everyone loves the upright bass, and you begin the Overture.

But, wait! Before all that happens, hopefully you reminded the orchestra at the final dress rehearsal of the following important considerations where performances are concerned:

If the orchestra is within view of the audience during the show, you need to make sure that whenever the orchestra is not playing music that they become invisible. Basically, nothing should be happening in the pit that will distract from what's happening on

Opening Night

stage. The musicians should become "neutral." Movement of any kind should be kept to a minimum. They should not be reading books, checking their phones, or conversing between musical numbers. I once attended a performance of *Hot Mikado* where the *conductor* could clearly be seen reading a paperback book between musical numbers. His level of engagement was inspiring. Oops, I'm sorry. Make that, distracting.

Musicians love to leave the gig as early as possible. What this can often mean on Closing Night is that a lot of musicians will start erasing any pencil marks in their parts right after each song is played. They will do this throughout the show. After they play the bows and exit music, they erase the few marks that are left, turn in their part, and hit the road. But what this means for the Closing Night audience is a lot of distractions. Erasing can be noisy; stands and stand lights tend to wiggle as the musicians quickly rub erasers across their parts. Noise and movement –

exactly what you *don't* want coming from the pit between songs. My rule for Closing Night when the orchestra is in plain view of the audience: erasing parts (which is mandatory) will take place only during intermission and after the show.

Speaking of stand lights, make sure they are angled so that audience members don't have the light bulbs shining in their eyes. As the conductor, it is important to consider everything from the perspective of an audience member. Think about the things you do and do not want to see or hear as you're trying to take in a show. Minimize distractions.

Okay, start the Overture! And as my mom always says: Don't forget to smile and have fun with it!

16

This I Believe

I believe American musical theatre is one of the most powerful, worthwhile art forms on earth. A single production has within it the potential to lift an audience to riotous laughter, to evoke tears, to fill people with hope, to motivate, to educate, to inspire – and all in the guise of "mere" entertainment. Musical theatre is a feast for the eyes and ears, the mind and heart.

As lofty as all that may sound, still, this art form relies on flesh-and-blood people to put it together and present it to a (hopefully) admiring crowd. But a problem has arisen within this art form that is slowly replacing warm bodies with cold, sterile technology, and eroding the fabric of blood, sweat, and tears that makes American musical theatre so great.

It is not enough to simply state that the electronic keyboard began wreaking havoc on the orchestra pit in the 60's and 70's, and that it's been downhill ever since. Nor is it enough to pine for the days when singers knew how to project and didn't need a battery pack stuffed down their pants and a microphone taped to their face. And while I could spend the rest of this essay deploring the ever-increasing use of canned music in community theatre productions and exhort everyone to call it what it is – karaoke – I think it is better to go right to the core of the problem, of which electronic keyboards, battery packs, and canned music are merely symptoms. The problem is that there are not enough musical theatre snobs.

American musical theatre began life in the shadow of European opera. You could say that musical theatre *is* opera – American-style. We like music and a good story like anyone else but, golly, can we just hear people talkin' sometimes? We wanted shows that were a little more down-to-earth, with a simpler style of music. We shed what we felt was the high-falutin' snobbery of grand opera.

I believe there are two kinds of snobbery: one is good, and one is bad. The bad kind of snobbery looks down on anything and anyone that isn't all about…well, whatever *it* may be. It's the opera lover who considers anything that is *not* opera to be second-rate. It's a form of arrogance.

The good kind of snobbery may be taken for the bad kind at first glance. "This is opera: we don't *use* mics. We use *real* violins, not the kind you hear coming out of a box with a keyboard attached to it. This is opera: we don't sing to a soundtrack." You can just hear the matronly woman in her mink coat with her slight British accent, her nose stuck in the air, her tone unapologetic. She might be a performer or a patron, we don't know. But look at what she is saying. Is she calling everything that isn't opera rubbish? No, she isn't making comparisons here. But she does, perhaps, seem a little defensive. If I didn't know any better, I'd say this person was trying to protect something. What is she trying to protect? Only *the integrity of an art form.* And it takes a certain kind of snobbery to protect it.

I believe it takes a bunch of devoted snobs to push back and say they love and admire their art form so much that they don't want to muddy it up, to cheapen it, to dilute it, to weaken it, to sterilize it, to make it "easy" to the point where you push a button and there it is. Opera lovers want an orchestra in the orchestra pit. As they file in and take their seats, opera lovers want to see string players – lots of them! – tightening their bows and playing scales to warm up. They want to hear the hall do what it was designed to do – to carry the human voice to their ears without an electronic intermediary. They want it straight from the actors' mouths and into their ears – simple, beautiful, powerful. They want the blood, sweat, and tears. It's worth it. It's so damn worth it!

I believe that since about the mid-1960's, especially where the orchestra pit is concerned, the attitude of "close enough" and "good enough" began to snowball in the musical theatre world – after all, this isn't grand opera! And in the last 50 years this attitude has become pervasive among the producers, directors, music directors, choreographers, actors, and audiences alike, both in the professional houses and in local community theatre. In those years we've seen steady advances in costuming, souped-up sound systems and set design (to the point of landing helicopters on stage), while the very element of musical theatre that provides the genre with its adjective – *music* – has declined pitifully, like an injured branch drying up on the vine. Instead of figuring out how many musicians we can put into the pit without breaking the fire code, we're always trying to see how few we can use *and still get away with it.*

And it keeps getting worse because we don't have the snobs among the producers, directors, music directors, choreographers, actors, and audiences to push back against the tide of mediocrity and preserve what opera lovers stubbornly cling to when it comes to their art – integrity.

I believe it's time for everyone who is involved with musical theatre, from patrons to producers, to start loving their art form with a renewed passion and pride, to love it with action and a healthy snobbery. I believe our art is not the "bastard child" of opera, but a proud and beautiful sister of equal standing. She deserves the richest costumes, the most dazzling sets, and the fullest orchestras that do justice to her music – her *music!* – some of the greatest music the world has ever produced. It's worth it. It's so damn worth it!

This I believe.

Index

Accompanist
    circle time, 119
    inexperienced, 82
    transposing, 22
Amplifier
    tweaking the sound, 87
Auditions
    avoiding long night, 17
    pianist, 17
    positive atmosphere, 14
    testing vocal ranges, 20

Bass
    acoustic vs. electric, 88

Casting, 21
Cello, 116
Choreography, 31
Closing Night
    erasing parts, 121
    see also: *Opening Night*

Conducting
    from the piano, 41
    formal training, 40
    Toscanini Syndrome, 43

Drums
    2-beat, 100, 108
    bass drum in swing beat, 102
    fills, 106
    hi-hat vs. cymbal, 105
    integrating Percussion book, 103, 106
    musical integrity, 29, 98
    swing, shuffle, and 12/8, 100

Electronic keyboard
    choosing "piano" sound, 84
    tweaking amplifier, 84

Index

Guitar
    following conductor, 85
    tweaking sound, 86

Music Director
    rehearsing cast, see: *Rehearsing*
    role in production, 8
Musical climax
    and staging, 34
Musical integrity, 29, 48
My mom, 122

Opening Night, 118
    see also: *Closing Night*

Orchestra
    balance, 60, 65
    placement, 58
    reduced orchestra, 54
    rehearsing, see: *Rehearsing*

Orchestra (continued)
    neutral between numbers, 120
    transposing, 22

Piano
    importance of left hand, 80
    piano vs. keyboard, 53
    piano/vocal score, 55, 56, 80
    taceting lines with orchestra, 83, 103

Rehearsing
    CAST
    adding choreography, 31
    enunciation, 28
    communication, 32
    have fun, 33
    musical integrity, 29
    scheduling, 25
    teaching music, 26

Index

Rehearsing (continued)
    CAST
    warm-ups, 26
    ORCHESTRA
    call time, 73
    consistency, 72
    delaying prep beat, 71
    fixing mistakes, 67
    measure numbers/reh. letters, 69
    one leader, 72
    rehearsal space, 68
    sit-and-sing, 73
    speaking clearly, 67

Score study
    know the story, 3
    recordings, 4
    reduced score, 4
Sound Designer, 63
Stand lights
    properly angled, 122

Strings
    keyboard substitute, 116
Style, see: *Musical integrity*

Trumpet
    in high register, 112
    use at least two, 55, 113
Tympani
    floor tom substitute, 106
    tuning, 115, 119

Vocals
    musical integrity, 29, 50
    projecting, 61
    transposing, 22

Woodwinds
    playing one book, 111
    in high register, 112

Printed in Great Britain
by Amazon